D0014418

With love,
Teddie

© 2004 by Barbour Publishing, Inc.

ISBN 1-59310-408-1

Cover image © GettyImages

Scripture quotations, unless otherwise noted, are taken from the King James Version of the Bible.

Scripture quotations marked NIV are taken from the HOLY BIBLE, NEW INTERNATIONAL VERSION®. NIV®. Copyright © 1973, 1978, 1984 by International Bible Society. Used by permission of Zondervan Publishing House. All rights reserved.

Published by Barbour Publishing, Inc., P.O. Box 719, Uhrichsville, Ohio 44683, www.barbourbooks.com

*Our mission is to publish and distribute inspirational products offering exceptional value and biblical encouragement to the masses.*

Printed in China.
5 4 3 2

# 'Tis the Season

### the

## Season

## Cathy Marie Hake

**DayMaker**

*Therefore the* **Lord** *himself*
*shall give you a sign;*

**Behold,** *a virgin shall conceive,*

*and bear a* **SON,**

*and shall call his name*

*Immanuel.*

ISAIAH 7:14

And Mary said, My soul doth magnify the Lord,
And my spirit hath rejoiced in God my Saviour.
For he hath regarded the low estate of his handmaiden:
for, behold, from henceforth
all generations shall call me blessed.
For he that is mighty hath done to me great things;
and holy is his name.

LUKE 1:46–49

'TIS THE
*Season*

# 'TIS THE *Season*

And Joseph also went up from Galilee,

out of the city of Nazareth, into Judaea,

unto the city of David,

which is called Bethlehem;

(because he was of the house and lineage of David:)

to be taxed with Mary his espoused wife,

being great with child.

LUKE 2:4–5

Mary was great with child. How weary she must have been! And Joseph—how much did he strive to hide the concern in his eyes as he walked alongside her? Faith and trust in the Lord kept them on the hard path.

What was the trip to Bethlehem like back in Bible times? Mary and Joseph traveled about seventy miles over rough roads, walking and using a small donkey as their transportation. It took them at least a full week to complete the journey.

7

# *Joseph* means

## *"God adds"* or *"God gathers."*

Can you imagine the responsibility of being chosen as guardian of the Redeemer?

### The Quiet Man of Christmas

Not one word of Joseph is recorded.
We only know what he did.
His actions speak far louder than words.

*'Tis the* Season

And so it was, that,
while they were there,
the days were accomplished that
she should be delivered.
And she brought forth
her firstborn son,
and wrapped him
in swaddling clothes,
and laid him in a manger;
because there was no room
for them in the inn.

LUKE 2:6–7

A strip of swaddling cloth and a borrowed stall
are such a humble welcome for the King.
The hope of mankind didn't come in majesty—
He came in utter humility. Lowly and meek,
He never changed in His approach, yet
He conquered the world, won our hearts,
and redeemed our souls.

9

'TIS THE *Season*

For unto us a child is born,
unto us a son is given:
and the government shall be
upon his shoulder:
and his name shall be called
Wonderful,
Counsellor,
The mighty God,
The everlasting Father,
The Prince of Peace.

ISAIAH 9:6

*God's gifts*
put man's
*best dreams*
to *shame.*

ELIZABETH BARRETT BROWNING

10

*Angels from the realms of glory,*
*wing your flight o'er all the earth...*

And there were in the same country shepherds abiding in the field, keeping watch over their flock by night. And, lo, the angel of the Lord came upon them, and the glory of the Lord shone round about them: and they were sore afraid.

LUKE 2:8–9

And the angel said unto them, Fear not: for, behold, I bring you good tidings of great joy, which shall be to all people. For unto you is born this day in the city of David a Saviour, which is Christ the Lord.

LUKE 2:10–11

*Ye who told creation's story,*
*now proclaim Messiah's birth...*

In
this was
manifested the

*love*

of God toward us,
because that God sent his
only begotten
Son into the world,
that we might live through him.

1 JOHN 4:9

*And this shall be a sign unto you;*
*Ye shall find the babe*
*wrapped in swaddling clothes,*
*lying in a manger.*

LUKE 2:12

# Humble King

Had You come in robes of light
And all of heaven's splendor
Instead of on a starry night,
I still might be a sinner.

For kings are far above my touch
And heaven was out of reach.
Humble folk could wish for much
Until You came to fill the breach.

Lowly cloths and borrowed bed
Were all this world would offer,
Yet heaven's wealth You gladly shed
To become my sweet Redeemer.

# 'TIS THE *Season*

And suddenly

there was with the angel

a multitude of the heavenly host praising God,

and saying, Glory to God in the highest,

and on earth peace, good will toward men.

LUKE 2:13–14

# *And it came to pass,*

as the angels were gone away from them into heaven,

the shepherds said one to another, Let us now go even unto

Bethlehem, and see this thing which is come to pass, which

the Lord hath made known unto us. And they came with haste,

and found Mary, and Joseph, and

## *the babe lying in a manger.*

LUKE 2:15–16

# Behold,

the Lamb of God
that taketh away
the sin of the *world!*

JOHN 1:29

*How fitting that the angels sent shepherds
to seek out the Lamb of Salvation!*

*"A star will come out of Jacob;*
*a scepter will rise out of Israel."*

NUMBERS 24:17 NIV

Where is he that is born King of the Jews?
for we have seen his star in the east,
and are come to worship him. . .
and, lo, the star, which they
saw in the east,
went before them,
till it came and stood over
where the young child was.
When they saw the star,
they rejoiced
with exceeding great joy.

MATTHEW 2:2, 9–10

'TIS THE
*Season*

O
Quiet
Night, one
Star so bright
Sentinel to the holy birth that night
By your light the Child came
Emmanuel, Christ Jesus
Is His holy name
Lullabies the angels sing
In heavenly love to the King
God has come to earth tonight
So beam your light
From above
Love is
Here.

'TIS THE *Season*

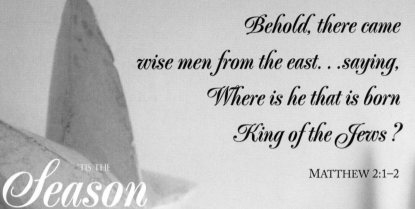

*Behold, there came wise men from the east. . .saying, Where is he that is born King of the Jews?*

MATTHEW 2:1–2

'TIS THE

*Season*

Until the wise men arrive, everyone in the Christmas story is of Abraham's lineage. God extended His grace and love to both Jew and Gentile alike.

When they saw the star, they rejoiced with exceeding great joy. And when they were come into the house, they saw the young child with Mary his mother, and fell down, and worshipped him.

MATTHEW 2:10–11

The real wisdom of the *Magi*

is not that they came to visit
the *Christ Child,*

but that once in

*His presence,*
they knelt and
*worshipped Him.*

It isn't enough to acknowledge

Christ's existence;

*He* must be accepted and *adored.*

The Magi were men of power,
rulers with great responsibilities
and obligations who put all of
life on hold to seek truth.

# *Season*

If we had *great wealth,*
would we have gone
to see if *Christ*
was the
*Promised One?*

And when they had
opened their treasures,
they presented unto him gifts;
gold,
and frankincense
and myrrh.

MATTHEW 2:11

21

*Gold*—the gift for a king.
It represented Christ's *royalty*.

*Frankincense*—
a tree resin burned by priests that
gave off a sweet smell.
It symbolized Christ's *deity* and role as our High Priest.

*Myrrh*—
a costly embalming fluid.
It foreshadowed the suffering, affliction,
and *death* of the Lamb of God.

But *Mary* kept
all these things,
and *pondered* them
in her *heart.*

LUKE 2:19

*God*-child

*Man*-child

She gave *You* life

So You can

give life to *all.*

*For God so loved the world...*

That
he
gave
his only begotten Son, that whosoever
believeth in him should not perish,
but have everlasting life.
For
God
sent not
his Son
into the
world to
condemn
the world;
but that
the world
through
him might be saved.
JOHN 3:16–17

'TIS THE *Season*

In
the
beginning
was the *Word,*
and the *Word* was
with *God,* and the
*Word* was *God.*
The
same was in the beginning with God. All things were
made by him; and without him was not any thing made
that was made. In him was life; and the life was the light
of men. And the light shineth in darkness; and the darkness comprehended it not. That was the true Light, which
lighteth every man that cometh into the world. He was
in the world, and the world was made by him, and the
world knew him not. He came unto his own, and his own
received him not. But as many as received him, to them
gave he power to become the sons of God, even to them
that believe on his name: Which were born, not of blood,
nor of the will of the flesh, nor of the will of man, but of
God. And the Word was made flesh, and dwelt among us,
(and we beheld his glory, the glory as of the only begotten of the Father,) full of grace and truth. JOHN 1:1–5, 9–14

# 'Tis the Season

'Tis the season to remember when

God came down to walk with men.

The Gift was not wrapped in boxes and bows

For mercy came in swaddling clothes.

So when you think of Christmastime

It isn't about trees and tinsel shine.

Love stepped down from heaven's height

And was born on earth that blessed night.

So pause sometime in December

For 'Tis the Season to remember.

# Joy to the World

Joy to the world! The Lord is come:
let earth receive her King!
Let every heart prepare Him room,
and heaven and nature sing.

Joy to the earth! the Saviour reigns:
let men their songs employ,
while fields and floods, rocks,
    hills and plains
repeat the sounding joy.

No more let sins and sorrows grow,
nor thorns infest the ground:
He comes to make His blessings flow
far as the curse is found.

He rules the earth with truth and grace,
and makes the nations prove
the glories of His righteousness
and wonders of His love.

ISAAC WATTS

*God's* divine *love*
has always met
man's every *need*—
and *He* continues
to be *faithful.*

# *Season*

In celebrating *Christmas,*

we revisit the *manger.*

It is the tangible reminder of the *prophecies*

and promises *Christ's* coming fulfilled.

How fitting that the

*One* who came to save and

nourish our *souls*

made *His* first bed in a feeding trough.

We only need to go

and partake of the

*bread of life* He

willingly *provides.*

In the quiet of the night
*You* spoke
In the sparkle of a star
*You* came
The humble shepherds
Bore witness
The wise and wealthy
Adored *You*
And centuries later,
The miracle is still fresh.
Welcome to my heart,
*Christ Jesus!*

'TIS THE
*Season*

What are we to make
of *Jesus Christ?*...
The real question is not
what we are to make of *Christ,*
but what is *He* to make of *us?*

C. S. LEWIS

'TIS THE

*Season*